IMAGES
of America

AROUND
SOUTHERN PINES
A SANDHILLS ALBUM
PHOTOGRAPHS BY E.C. EDDY

Participants in a fox hunt ride slowly along a sandy road near Southern Pines in the 1930s. The master of the hounds, James Boyd (1888–1944), is the rider on the far left in the lead group. Boyd, a gifted novelist and resident of Southern Pines, along with his brother, Jackson H. Boyd (1892–1984), co-founded the fox-hunting club known as Moore County Hounds in 1914. (Courtesy of North Carolina Division of Archives and History.)

IMAGES
of America

AROUND
SOUTHERN PINES
A SANDHILLS ALBUM
PHOTOGRAPHS BY E.C. EDDY

Stephen E. Massengill

ARCADIA

First published 1998
Copyright © Stephen E. Massengill, 1998

ISBN 0-7524-0951-4

Published by Arcadia Publishing,
an imprint of the Chalford Publishing Corporation,
One Washington Center, Dover, New Hampshire 03820.
Printed in Great Britain

Library of Congress Cataloging-in-Publication Data applied for

Shown above is an example of a greeting card variety of postcard produced by E.C. Eddy in the 1920s. This one contains a pine bough, the state flag, and the state slogan. (Courtesy of Willard E. Jones.)

Contents

Acknowledgments

E.C. Eddy's photographs have appeared in several publications about the history of Southern Pines during the last two decades. The majority of images included within this work, however, have never been published. The person who has made the greatest contribution to this publication is Ellenore Eddy Smith, the only surviving daughter of E.C. Eddy. She greatly admired her father and openly shared with me her memories of his early life in Moore County. Mrs. Smith supplied about one-quarter of the pictures used in this volume and made available to me some interesting hand-written recollections by her father of his earliest days in Pinehurst and Southern Pines. Details from E.C. Eddy's personal reminiscences have been incorporated into a portion of the picture captions.

Other individuals and institutions that provided images for reproduction in this book include Durwood Barbour, Bob W. Brendle, Eric H. Dovre, the Rare Book, Manuscript, and Special Collections Library at Duke University, the First Savings Bank of Southern Pines, B.T. Fowler, Aubrey T. Haddock, Gene Hamlin, Willard E. Jones, the North Carolina Collection, the North Carolina Division of Archives and History, Tony Parker, Sarah M. Pope, and the Tufts Archives in Pinehurst.

Others who helped with the completion of this work include Alexander Boyd, James Vann Comer, Jerry Cotten, Ray Garlow, Bill Garrett, Leigh H. Gunn, Faye Hamlin, the staff of LK Copy Center in Southern Pines, Reid A. Page Jr., Tom Parramore, the staff of the Southern Pines *Pilot*, William Samuels, the staff of the State Library of North Carolina, the staff of Turner Printing Services, Alan L. Westmoreland, and the staff of Weymouth Center for the Arts and Humanities in Southern Pines.

Special gratitude is extended to Durwood Barbour, a good friend with a vast collection of North Carolina postcards, who shared his collection with me and encouraged me to compile a book on E.C. Eddy's works. Heartfelt thanks is directed to local residents Faye Dasen, Norris Hodgkins, Khristine E. Januzik, Tony Parker, and Richard J. Schloegl, who gave invaluable assistance to an outsider. Also, I wish to acknowledge the late Sara W. Hodgkins for her leadership role in state and local cultural affairs. I am certain that she admired the work of Eddy and was glad that some of it survived to document past times in Moore County.

I direct my sincere appreciation to my special friend Robert M. Topkins, who edited the manuscript and prepared the index. I am grateful to my wife, Caroline Warren Massengill, and our daughters Carla and Stacey for their support throughout this endeavor.

I dedicate this volume to Ellenore Eddy Smith, whose valuable contributions helped make this book a reality. I deeply appreciate her patient hospitality and assistance during the project, and I thank her for allowing me to share her father's life story and publish a portion of his outstanding photographs in this pictorial work.

Introduction

Ellsworth Curtis Eddy (1882–1969), a son of Peter (1847–1925) and Mary Wheeler (1849–1900) Eddy, was born in the community of Hollis in southern New Hampshire. E.C. Eddy received his given name in honor of Union general Elmer Ephraim Ellsworth (1837–1861), an early casualty during the Civil War. Peter Eddy worked as a photographer in New Hampshire during the last quarter of the nineteenth century, when photo artists employed glass-plate negatives and mixed their own developing chemicals. Young Eddy during his early years gained an interest in that profession.

After completing his formal education in the public schools of New Hampshire, Eddy was employed as a photographer during the tourist season in the White Mountains of his home state. He and his father took pictures of passengers on the train that traveled to the top of Mount Washington. While in the White Mountains, he met photographer and businessman Edmond L. Merrow (c. 1861–1922), a native of Maine, who hired him to work at a resort near Mount Washington. Merrow had worked in Bethlehem, New Hampshire, for 14 consecutive summers and was considered to be one of the finest photographers in New England. In the winter of 1900, Merrow began to operate a photo gallery in Pinehurst, North Carolina.

During the fall and winter months, Eddy worked in a grocery store and shoe store at East Hartford, Connecticut, and studied business at a night school in Boston. While attending a square dance in Boston, he met Alice Crosby (1881–1973), a native of Nova Scotia, and the two were married on May 24, 1906.

Merrow enticed Eddy to travel to Pinehurst in the fall of 1907 to assist him in his photograph studio. During the following four winters, Eddy apprenticed under Merrow in Pinehurst, processing film and taking outdoor pictures, primarily of golfers and horseback riders. For advertising purposes, he also took photographs of any visitors of note to the resort. During the summer seasons between 1907 and 1910, Eddy returned to Fabyan (near Bethlehem), New Hampshire, to photograph vacationers in the White Mountains.

Eddy came again to Pinehurst in the fall of 1910. Although he liked photography and had learned a great deal about the profession from Merrow, he was forced to accept another position because the $17 he earned per week was not enough to support his family. Eddy rented saddle horses at a livery stable to guests of the Carolina Hotel. After his annual summer trip to New Hampshire, Eddy removed to Southern Pines in the fall of 1912 to operate the New Haven House. After struggling to break even at that Broad Street boardinghouse, Eddy decided to return to the photography profession on a permanent basis. On May 21, 1913, he purchased studio stock and equipment from photographer I.E. Goodale of Southern Pines for $750. Since most of the area's tourists had left for the North, Eddy stored his newly acquired equipment and traveled back to New Hampshire for the summer.

The following fall, the Eddy family returned to Southern Pines to begin their commercial photography venture. Eddy arranged his new quarters and erected a painted background in the studio to allow him to engage in portraiture. He also photographed local scenes that he thought would sell as photo postcards. The space that he rented for his studio was in the Locey Block, a business building on Pennsylvania Avenue owned by a retired attorney and judge named George H. Locey (b. 1841).

Eddy worked hard to build a loyal following and became a leading member of the community. He belonged to the Southern Pines Masonic Lodge and played an active role in the Church of Wide Fellowship (formerly a Congregational church). He photographed many famous visitors to the resorts, including sculptor Gutzon Borglum, aviatrix Amelia Earhart, jurist Charles Evans Hughes, performers Annie Oakley and Will Rogers, puppeteer Tony Sarg, bandleader and composer John Philip Sousa, and singer Gladys Swarthout. He undertook assignments for local prominent families such as the Boyds, Pages, and Tufts. Newspapers in New York purchased Eddy's photographs of Southern Pines to publish in conjunction with their advertisements for the resort.

Many of Eddy's early images were not marked with his name, and other enterprising local merchants purchased his photographs, reproduced them on postcards, and sold the cards in their stores. Among the firms that took credit for some of Eddy's initial work were Hayes's Bookstore (operated by Southern Pines merchant Charles L. Hayes); Charles Cole & Company, a drugstore and bookstore in Carthage; and the Fox Drug Company in Aberdeen.

In April 1921, a disastrous fire destroyed Eddy's studio along with several other businesses located at or near the corner of Pennsylvania Avenue and Broad Street. Soon thereafter, Eddy constructed a two-story brick edifice on Pennsylvania Avenue to house his business. He rented vacant space in the building to other merchants in the town.

E.C. and Alice Eddy had three children—Doris (1907–1995), Ellenore (b. 1919), and Alice "Sukey" (1924–1979). They resided on East Massachusetts Avenue in a two-story wood-frame house to which Eddy later added a wing for a studio. The brick building that housed the studio and the house still stand but are no longer owned by the family. Doris Eddy studied at a school for professional photographers and often assisted her father in the studio and tediously hand-colored many of his photographs with watercolors. She also originated the catchy slogan "photograph the present for future memories of the past," which was printed on studio stationery.

Here, in an unusual occurrence, the photographer gets photographed! Eddy focuses his hand-held camera on riders at an equestrian event in Moore County in the 1930s. The horses may be participants in the popular equestrian games known as Gymkhana. (Courtesy of Ellenore Eddy Smith.)

Eddy's enterprise continued to flourish during the prosperous years between the end of World War I and the Great Depression. The reputation of Southern Pines as an established health resort brought increased development to the town. Eddy's business, as well as most others in Southern Pines, suffered during the depression years, however. The resort trade declined, and business was extremely slow. Eddy's rental property, investments, and sporadic tourist-related activity enabled him to make it through the hard times.

World War II helped the economy of Southern Pines and the Sandhills recover as military-related projects connected with Fort Bragg brought more residents to the town. Eddy remained in business until 1945, when he sold his studio to photographer Emerson Humphrey (c. 1905–1979). The Eddys retired and moved to Florida, but they continued to drive to New Hampshire every summer to spend time with their daughters and grandchildren. E.C. Eddy enjoyed more than two decades of retirement before his death at New Port Richey, Florida, on June 30, 1969.

E.C. Eddy labored as a photographer in Moore County for 38 years. It is through the medium of postcards that many of his images survive today. Many fine examples of his work are found in accumulations of postcard collectors throughout the country. Additional samples of his pictures are preserved in scrapbooks of his descendants, in holdings of private collectors, and in local historical collections. Moreover, many treasured family portraits taken by Eddy are retained by descendants of former residents of Moore County. Eddy's efforts documented life in the Sandhills during the first four decades of the century. He was a hardworking, honest, caring man who loved people, his town, and his profession. Those traits helped Eddy become an outstanding photographer and one of the leaders in the field in North Carolina during the first half of the twentieth century.

Above is a charming portrait of the Eddy family in New Hampshire in the late 1880s. Front row, left to right, are Mabel, Marcia, and Ellsworth (E.C.); (second row) Ackland, Mary (E.C.'s mother), Wellington, Peter (E.C.'s father), and Floyd. (Courtesy of Ellenore Eddy Smith.)

Eddy proudly shows off his first automobile for the camera about 1915. He purchased the car from a woman who had won it in a lottery. In the vehicle behind Eddy, left to right, are Alice Crosby Eddy (his wife), Suze Crosby (his sister-in-law), Bernice Henry (his niece), Winnie Crosby Henry (his sister-in-law), and Doris Eddy (his daughter). (Courtesy of Durwood Barbour.)

Firemen of the Southern Pines Volunteer Fire Department pose with their firetruck in front of Eddy's Photograph Studio on Pennsylvania Avenue near Northwest Broad Street in the late 1910s. Also behind the fire engine is the jewelry and watch-repair business of Harry F. Howe. Fire destroyed the building in 1921. (Courtesy of Ellenore Eddy Smith.)

Reproduced here is a self-portrait of the profile of E.C. Eddy taken about 1920. (Courtesy of Ellenore Eddy Smith.)

For many years this residence on East Massachusetts Avenue was the home of the Eddy family in Southern Pines. Subsequently, Eddy added a wing to the right side of the house to serve as a studio. The dwelling still stands but is no longer owned by the family. (Courtesy of Ellenore Eddy Smith.)

11

Eddy and his camera stand atop his wooden scaffold in front of the Highland Pines Inn shortly after its construction in 1912. Eddy used the structure to capture bird's-eye views around Southern Pines and vicinity. (Courtesy of Ellenore Eddy Smith.)

Along with his daughter Doris, Eddy poses for the camera near the Carolina Hotel in Pinehurst about 1911. Two of Eddy's toughest photographic assignments involved the hotel. He had to balance on the chimney of a nearby cottage to get an exterior view of the front of the building. In addition, Eddy successfully undertook a lengthy exposure of the desk and lobby inside the hotel. (Courtesy of Ellenore Eddy Smith.)

Eddy constructed this two-story brick studio (at left) on Pennsylvania Avenue near Broad Street shortly after a fire destroyed his gallery in 1921. The Hart Building stands to the right of his studio. (Courtesy of Ellenore Eddy Smith.)

Shown here is a close-up picture of Eddy's studio in the 1930s. He rented the left side of the building to various tenants. At the time this photograph was made, a beauty shop was in business on the first floor. (Courtesy of Ellenore Eddy Smith.)

One
Pinehurst

Spectators fill the grandstand and crowd together along the rail to watch a horse race at the track at Pinehurst in the late 1910s. (Courtesy of North Carolina Collection, University of North Carolina Library, Chapel Hill.)

Edmond L. Merrow opened this photographic studio between the General Store and the Magnolia Inn at Pinehurst in 1901. Merrow had worked as a photographer at the resort village for several winter seasons and had gained a favorable reputation. In the fall of 1907, Merrow hired Eddy to come south as an assistant in the studio at Pinehurst. Eddy had previously driven a Pierce-Arrow automobile for Merrow during the summers at a resort in the White Mountains of New Hampshire. Eddy worked with Merrow through the 1910 season. (Courtesy of Tufts Archives, Pinehurst.)

"The Carolina" Pinehurst, N. C.

PUBL. BY E.C. EDDY

Eddy published a photograph of the Carolina Hotel at Pinehurst on this postcard in the early 1920s. The Carolina Hotel was constructed during 1899–1900 and was the centerpiece of tourism in the resort village for many years. One of Eddy's most difficult tasks was taking a panoramic view with a glass-plate negative from the cupola of the hotel. (Courtesy of Sarah M. Pope.)

Alice Crosby Eddy and daughter Doris pose for Eddy's camera near the entrance to the Carolina Hotel about 1911. Eddy's wife and firstborn daughter were favorite subjects of his early photographs at Pinehurst. (Courtesy of Ellenore Eddy Smith.)

The Merrow Studio photographed these horseback riders at an outdoor circus performance near the Carolina Hotel about the time that Merrow employed Eddy. (Courtesy of Sarah M. Pope.)

Spectators view the entertaining games on horseback known as Gymkhana on the side lawn of the Carolina Hotel in the 1910s. Contestants competed in a variety of events to display their skills, as well as those of the horses. (Courtesy of Durwood Barbour.)

Eddy captured this view of a pageant at the Sandhills Fair from the grandstand of the racetrack at Pinehurst. This unique folk gathering for Moore County was held every fall and included a pageant, parade, and livestock show. (Courtesy of North Carolina Collection.)

Merrow assigned Eddy to photograph the first Curtiss biplane to arrive at Pinehurst. Daring exhibition pilot Lincoln Beachey (1887–1915) brought his Curtiss "pusher" to the village in March 1911. The *Buzz Buzzard* was assembled in a field near the trapshooting grounds. (Courtesy of Ellenore Eddy Smith.)

Perhaps Eddy's most challenging assignment was to take aerial photographs of Pinehurst as a passenger in Beachey's biplane. Eddy and his camera were airborne for 25 minutes on March 25, and he took four good snapshots. One of the aerial views, reproduced here on a postcard, shows the cottage of Mrs. Hurd in the foreground, the Holly Inn at back center, and the Berkshire Hotel on the left. It is believed to be the first aerial photograph taken in North Carolina. (Courtesy of Ellenore Eddy Smith.)

This postcard view shows the clubhouse at Pinehurst Country Club about 1910. Famed golf course architect Donald J. Ross (1872–1948) designed the golf courses (three were in operation at that time). (Courtesy of Gene Hamlin.)

Caddies and golfers mingle near the clubhouse of the Pinehurst Country Club about 1916. The building had been enlarged a couple of times during the early 1900s. The facility became the winter golfing center of the nation after World War I. (From the author's collection.)

Women shooters display their skills on the rifle range at the Pinehurst Gun Club about 1910. Contestants shot at targets attached to lines extending out from hand cranks on the sides of the wooden stands. (Courtesy of Ellenore Eddy Smith.)

A large crowd has assembled at this picturesque log cabin, home of the Pinehurst Gun Club, to witness a trapshooting match about 1909. The Merrow Studio published the photograph on a picture postcard. (Courtesy of Gene Hamlin.)

Eddy positioned himself trackside to get this picture of a trotting race at the Pinehurst track in the late 1910s. The facility also hosted horse racing, steeplechases, and polo matches. (Courtesy of Ellenore Eddy Smith.)

Trotting Race   Pinehurst, N. C.

This is a close-up view of trotters during a race at the Pinehurst track. Eddy placed this photograph on a postcard in the 1920s. (Courtesy of Postcard Collection, Rare Books, Manuscript, and Special Collections Library, Duke University.)

Dogs often performed for the public in shows sponsored by the Pinehurst Kennel Club. Here a trainer coaxes a canine over a wooden barrier at the Pinehurst track in the 1910s. (Courtesy of Ellenore Eddy Smith.)

Much to the delight of onlookers, a trained bear sits in a chair in front of the Carolina Hotel about 1909. The trainer has a tether fastened around the neck of the animal as a safety measure. (Courtesy of Ellenore Eddy Smith.)

Two

Southern Pines: The "Capital of Sunshineland"

Eddy achieved this slightly elevated view of the corner of West New Hampshire Avenue and Northwest Broad Street about 1915. Townspeople mingle and stroll along Broad Street. The Jefferson Inn on New Hampshire Avenue is visible in the center of the picture. (Courtesy of Willard E. Jones.)

Eddy climbed to the top of a building to get this photograph of Southern Pines about 1915. A mule-drawn wagon moves north on Northeast Broad Street. In the background are buildings on West Broad Street near Pennsylvania Avenue. (Courtesy of Durwood Barbour.)

Alice Eddy (with parasol) and daughter Doris take a leisurely stroll on Northwest Broad Street in Southern Pines about 1911. This is about the time that the family moved from Pinehurst to Southern Pines. (Courtesy of Ellenore Eddy Smith.)

This Eddy postcard contains a glimpse of a residential section of New Hampshire Avenue looking west from the eastern heights of Southern Pines in the 1910s. A tall flagpole stands in the middle of the intersection of North Ashe Street and New Hampshire Avenue. (Courtesy of Aubrey T. Haddock.)

West Broad Street.   Southern Pines, N. C.

Shown here is a street-level view of Northwest Broad Street, looking south between Connecticut Avenue and New Hampshire Avenue in the 1920s. At left is the Seaboard Air Line Railroad Depot, which had been completed about 1900. (Courtesy of Willard E. Jones.)

Eddy recorded this panoramic view of the town from a rooftop across from the Southern Pines

A military band leads a march northward along Northwest Broad Street in Southern Pines during an Armistice Day parade in November about 1921. (Courtesy of First Savings Bank of Southern Pines; William Samuels, president.)

Hotel on March 1, 1916. His camera was pointed almost due north. (Courtesy of the North Carolina Collection.)

The department store of Cephus Taylor Patch (c. 1869–1946) dominates this view of Northwest Broad Street between New Hampshire Avenue and Pennsylvania Avenue in the late 1920s. Patch's store dates from 1909, and the adjacent structure on the right is the Valentine Building (1927), which Patch acquired for his expanding business. (Courtesy of Tony Parker.)

Two unidentified men give E.C. Eddy a warm send-off before he boards an airplane to take aerial views of Southern Pines in 1920. Nine years earlier, Eddy had flown over Pinehurst with his camera in Lincoln Beachey's *Buzz Buzzard*. (Courtesy of Ellenore Eddy Smith.)

Just prior to takeoff, Eddy discusses plans with the pilot in the cockpit of the airplane owned by the Colonial Aerial Transportation Company. (Courtesy of Ellenore Eddy Smith.)

Shown here is one of the successful bird's-eye photographs of Southern Pines recorded by Eddy in 1920. This view, looking southwest, shows most of the business district of the growing town between Pennsylvania Avenue and Connecticut Avenue. New Hampshire Avenue intersects Northwest Broad Street near the center of the picture. The Seaboard Air Line Railroad Depot stands just west of the railroad tracks. (From the author's collection.)

Spectators line both sides of Broad Street in anticipation of the parade during the Firemen's Carnival held in Southern Pines, March 23–26, 1915. The town honored its firefighters with decorated storefronts and floats. (Courtesy of Durwood Barbour.)

Businessmen and townspeople pose in front of the Tarbell Building on Broad Street during the Firemen's Carnival in March 1915. Left to right are Ashley Jackman, Alex Fields Sr., Sam B. Richardson, S.A. Richardson, C.T. Patch, a boy who may be Charles Kimball, Irving Hamlin, an unidentified African-American man, ? Loomis, two unidentified men, an unidentified African-American boy, and Dolph Ruggles. (Courtesy of First Savings Bank of Southern Pines.)

Seven riders sit in this attractively adorned automobile, which served as a float in the parade during the festivities of the Firemen's Carnival. (Courtesy of Durwood Barbour.)

This is an Eddy photograph of the guests of honor as they march in the parade in 1915. The firemen are members of the No. 1 Reel Company of Southern Pines. On the far left is Edward Ruggles, the youngest member of the fire department. (Courtesy of Gene Hamlin.)

Boy Scout Troop 2 of Southern Pines poses in front of its cabin on the corner of Connecticut Avenue and Ashe Street in the early 1920s. The troop was formed in 1914. (Courtesy of First Savings Bank of Southern Pines.)

Girl Scouts of Southern Pines are pictured here in a vehicle decorated with stars and stripes and pine boughs in the early 1920s. The first troop had been established in 1918. (Courtesy of First Savings Bank of Southern Pines.)

Charles W. Picquet (d. 1957) opened the Princess Theater on Northeast Broad Street in February 1914. It provided live theater and first-run movies for nearly 40 years. The front facade of the landmark was changed to a pitched roof in the 1920s. (Courtesy of Willard E. Jones.)

Eddy brought his camera indoors to get this photograph of the Tea Tray, a tearoom on May Street in Southern Pines in the 1920s. He published this interior view on a postcard, and a female customer mailed it on April 1, 1926, to a woman in Los Angeles, California, with the following message: "This is Miss Parker's tea room. I have been here for a little visit with her and we have been talking a lot about you. She is as nice as her brother." (Courtesy of Willard E. Jones.)

Here is an early-1910s photograph of the First Baptist Church on Page Street in Southern Pines. Workers constructed the main sanctuary in 1899, and the bell tower and lecture rooms were added in 1904. Members worshiped in this building until 1936. The structure subsequently served as a school and apartments. (Courtesy of Sarah M. Pope.)

Eddy stepped inside the First Baptist Church to get this interior photograph of the front of the sanctuary and pulpit in the 1910s. (Courtesy of Willard E. Jones.)

Pictured here is St. Anthony's Catholic Church, which was situated at the corner of Vermont Avenue and Ashe Street. It had its beginnings as a mission church in 1895. (Courtesy of Willard E. Jones.)

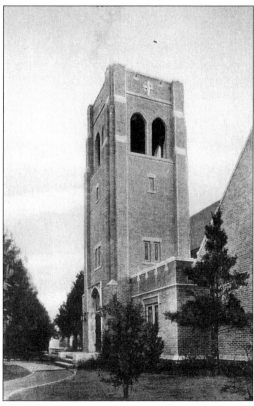

The focus of this c. 1920s picture postcard is the bell tower of the Church of Wide Fellowship (formerly a Congregational church) and currently the Community Congregational Church of Southern Pines. Eddy and his family were members of the congregation. The church is located on the corner of New Hampshire Avenue and Bennett Street. (Courtesy of Willard E. Jones.)

The Southern Pines Graded School was completed in 1908 on the block bordered by Ridge Street, New York Avenue, and Massachusetts Avenue. The building later served as the high school for Moore County and is now the site of a middle school. (Courtesy of Willard E. Jones.)

This postcard by Eddy, postmarked January 24, 1927, shows the building that replaced the 1908 facility as the graded school for elementary students in 1924. (Courtesy of Willard E. Jones.)

Eddy published this scene along West Broad Street in Southern Pines on a postcard about 1920. The photographer has "touched up" this picture postcard, and it does not reflect the realism exhibited in the photograph of a similar view shown below. (Courtesy of Durwood Barbour.)

A lone car moves southward on Broad Street near New Hampshire Avenue in the early 1920s. The buildings, from the center of block, from left to right, are the Leavitt Building, the Arcade, Patch's Department Store, and the Citizens Bank. Eddy was positioned near the railroad depot when he took the photograph. (Courtesy of Ellenore Eddy Smith.)

From 1904 to 1937, the post office of Southern Pines occupied the first floor of the building at the corner of Broad Street and Pennsylvania Avenue. This building also housed the popular Belvedere Hotel, which had its lobby entrance on Pennsylvania Avenue and rooms on the second floor. (Courtesy of Durwood Barbour.)

West Broad Street   Southern Pines, N. C.

This Eddy photograph of West Broad Street at Pennsylvania Avenue was printed on a postcard in the early 1930s. At left is the Hart Building, completed in 1926, and in the distance on the right is the railroad station. (Courtesy of Sarah M. Pope.)

Southeast Broad Street Southern Pines, N C

Eddy pointed his camera north along northeast Broad Street to get this exposure in the mid-1920s. On the right are the Schemmler Building, which at one time included a casino and bowling alley, and the Princess Theater (to the left of the vacant lot). (Courtesy of Durwood Barbour.)

NEW HAMPSHIRE AVENUE.
SOUTHERN PINES, N. C.

A tree-lined median divides New Hampshire Avenue in this c. 1920 view looking west from Broad Street. On the left is the Jefferson Inn, which had been enlarged in 1912. (Courtesy of Sarah M. Pope.)

41

The *Southern Pines Tourist* began publication as a weekly newspaper in 1903. In this view, taken about 1911, the newspaper and printing business is situated in Sadelson's Building at 190 West Pennsylvania Avenue. Dr. Robert E. Foss (d. 1920), a local minister, edited the paper, which changed its name to the *Sandhill Citizen* in 1915. (Courtesy of Eric H. Dovre.)

Riders on horseback pose for Eddy at the Firemen's Carnival held in Southern Pines in March 1915. The group probably marched in the parade. (Courtesy of Durwood Barbour.)

Three
Accommodations for Tourists

This real-photo postcard features huntsman Harry Knott "roading" the hounds near the entrance of the Belvedere Hotel on Pennsylvania Avenue in the late 1920s. The landmark two-story brick hostelry opened in Southern Pines in 1917. (Courtesy of Willard E. Jones.)

Allison Francis Page (1824–1899), who left Cary and settled in Moore County in 1881, erected the Southern Pines Hotel in 1887. The town's first resort hotel was situated on Broad Street between New York and Pennsylvania Avenues. It was enlarged about the turn of the century and was destroyed by fire in 1931. (Courtesy of Willard E. Jones.)

The New England House on New York Avenue in Southern Pines was constructed in 1897 as a residence and boardinghouse for Samuel J. Whipple of Vermont. Originally called the Vermont House, it briefly served as a hospital for Moore County. Here a group of lodgers poses on the first- and second-floor porches about 1917. (Courtesy of Durwood Barbour.)

The Jefferson Inn opened as a boardinghouse on New Hampshire Avenue in Southern Pines in 1901. The hotel was expanded and reopened as the New Jefferson Inn in 1912. Shown here is an exterior view of the three-story structure in the late 1920s. (Courtesy of Sarah M. Pope.)

This is a rare interior photograph of the first floor of the New Jefferson Inn. Eddy probably took the picture in the 1920s. Clearly visible are the furnishings, fixtures, and steam radiator heater in the lobby. (From the author's collection.)

Reproduced here is an unusual panoramic view of the Southland Hotel in Southern Pines in the 1920s. The New Hampshire Avenue hostelry opened for the tourist trade in 1892 as the

The Southland.   Southern Pines, N. C.

When Eddy published this postcard, the hotel was known as the Southland and had been more than doubled in size (addition at left). The old hotel was razed in 1972. (Courtesy of Willard E. Jones.)

Ozone and later was known as Oak Hall before finally being named the Southland. (From the author's collection.)

The tables are set and prepared for guests in the dining room of the Southland Hotel about 1920. The inn specialized in fine meals for the traveling public. (From the author's collection.)

New York architect Aymar Embury II designed the Highland Pines Inn in the Colonial Revival style. Completed in 1912 on upper Massachusetts Avenue in Southern Pines, it provided recreational and resort activities for important visitors for many seasons. Eddy took this distant view from the west side of the winding road to the hotel. (Courtesy of Sarah M. Pope.)

Reproduced here on a postcard is a close-up view of the eastern section of the Highland Pines Inn in the 1920s. The inn served as a center for cultural life in the town for several decades. The person who mailed the postcard remarked that "the prices here would make your hair curl." Fire destroyed the famous hotel in 1957. (Courtesy of Sarah M. Pope.)

Golfers complete a hole at the Mid Pines Country Club, a few miles west of Southern Pines, in the late 1920s. The resort hotel, including an 18-hole golf course designed by Donald J. Ross, opened in 1921. The military took over the facility during World War II. (Courtesy of First Savings Bank of Southern Pines.)

Eddy placed two photographs on this souvenir postcard of the Pinebluff Inn about 1919. The original resort opened at Pinebluff in 1903 and remained in use until replaced by a more modern structure in 1925. At left visitors pose on horseback near the inn, while on the right a cook displays a turkey for the camera. (Courtesy of Durwood Barbour.)

One of the first grand houses built on East Rhode Island Avenue extension in Southern Pines was Hedgerow. The Colonial Revival style residence was constructed in 1900 for the Elisha Fulton family. A subsequent owner added 20 rooms and operated it as a small hotel known as Cedar Pines Villa. By 1927 the building was renovated by new owners and renamed Hibernia. (Courtesy of Bob W. Brendle.)

E.C. Eddy took this aerial view of Southern Pines from the east in 1920. In the left center of the photograph is the Hollywood Hotel. It opened in 1913 just off New York Avenue and could accommodate 200 guests. (From the author's collection.)

Pictured here is a close-up view of the Hollywood Hotel soon after it opened for tourists. Eddy often photographed the popular hostelry, which stood until 1966. (Courtesy of Bob W. Brendle.)

Eddy published this real-photo postcard of the Pine Needles Inn about the time the resort opened in January 1928. The Tudor design resort near Southern Pines ran into financial difficulty during the depression years and never fully recovered. The Army Air Force Technical Training Command was headquartered in the hotel during World War II. In 1948, the inn was converted into a hospital and sanatorium named St. Joseph of the Pines. (Courtesy of Durwood Barbour.)

In the 1910s, Eddy placed this view of the Gould Apartment Buildings in Southern Pines on a postcard. L.A. Gould built and operated boardinghouses on North May Street for resort residents with a more moderate income. (Courtesy of Durwood Barbour.)

The New Haven House on the corner of Broad Street and Massachusetts Avenue in Southern Pines serves as the backdrop in this photograph of Alice and Doris Eddy about 1912. The Eddy family operated the boardinghouse during the 1912–1913 season. The house contained 11 rooms, 2.5 baths, 7 fireplaces, and a wood furnace. After struggling to break even, Eddy soon decided to resume his career in photography in Southern Pines. (Courtesy of Ellenore Eddy Smith.)

Four

Sports and Recreation in the Sandhills

Spectators encircle a sand green to watch golfers putt during a tournament at Southern Pines Country Club before 1920. At that time, greens were covered with sand instead of grass. Eddy photographed numerous amateur and professional golfers in the Sandhills and even took up the game of golf himself in the fall of 1909. (Courtesy of North Carolina Collection.)

A female golfer prepares to tee off on the first hole of Course No. 1 at Pinehurst in the 1910s. African-American caddies and a small group of onlookers watch near a wooden table that contains sand, which players used to form tees on which to place golf balls. The E.L. Merrow Studio of Pinehurst produced the postcard. (Courtesy of Sarah M. Pope.)

Country Club. Southern Pines, N. C.

A tournament competitor drives from a tee at the Southern Pines Country Club in the 1910s. Donald J. Ross designed the links, completing the first nine holes in 1910. The clubhouse and back nine opened in 1912. (Courtesy of Willard E. Jones.)

54

The Southern Pines Country Club is the setting for this tournament, held about 1919. A golfer follows through as he watches his drive travel down the fairway. The round receptacle near the golfer holds the tee sand. (Courtesy of Gene Hamlin.)

A small gallery intently watches the tee shot of a player in a tournament at Southern Pines about 1920. The golfer, as are some of the onlookers, is dressed in knickers. At that time the tee boxes, like the greens, were covered with sand. (Courtesy of Sarah M. Pope.)

Eddy directs his camera toward the action on a small sand putting green at Southern Pines about 1920. On the heights beyond the golfers is the Highland Pines Inn. (Courtesy of Tony Parker.)

Pictured here is a distant view of golfers on a putting surface at Pinebluff Country Club in the 1920s. The building behind the green is the clubhouse. (Courtesy of Gene Hamlin.)

A foursome stands on the putting green at Southern Pines Country Club in the 1910s. A young African-American caddie dressed in knickers holds the bag of one of the competitors. (Courtesy of Gene Hamlin.)

For this photograph, made in the 1920s, Eddy positioned his camera behind a gallery of well-dressed golf fans to shoot tournament action on a green at the Southern Pines Country Club. (Courtesy of North Carolina Collection.)

Off to the Hunt   Southern Pines, N. C.

Fox hunters and their pack of hounds travel on Morganton Road in front of the historic Shaw House at Southern Pines in the early 1920s. The Boyd family's Moore County Hounds is the oldest formal fox-hunt club in the state. (Courtesy of Gene Hamlin.)

Hunters leaving Highland Pines Inn.   Southern Pines, N. C.

The scene depicted on this Eddy postcard features fox hunters leaving Highland Pines Inn at Southern Pines on their way to the hunting field. The hotel's proximity to the hunt country and its excellent riding stables allowed guests to participate in this equestrian activity. (Courtesy of Willard E. Jones.)

A pack of foxhounds and hunters strike out on a hunt in the 1930s from Weymouth, the estate of the Boyd family at Southern Pines. Eddy admitted that one of his most difficult photograph assignments was mounting a horse with a camera to take pictures of a fox hunt. He failed to get any pictures, and the only result "was the necessity of carrying a pillow to put in every chair [he] sat in for a week." (Courtesy of the North Carolina Division of Archives and History.)

The young hunter at right displays the results of a successful fox hunt in this real-photo postcard taken near Southern Pines in the 1920s. (Courtesy of Ellenore Eddy Smith.)

On this postcard, captioned "After the Chase," a hunter holds a dead fox above his head, to the delight of hunters and hounds alike. (Courtesy of Gene Hamlin.)

At left, hunters pose with their hounds during a drag hunt near Southern Pines about 1916. In this sport, the huntsman sets a cross-country course by dragging a bag containing a scent for the hounds and riders to follow. (Courtesy of Durwood Barbour.)

The masters of the hunt lead the "field" on its return trip following an exhilarating hunt in Weymouth Heights near Southern Pines about 1925. (Courtesy of Durwood Barbour.)

Sportsman Stanley Burke (at right), wearing a top hat, sits atop a well-bred mount at an equestrian event at Southern Pines in the 1930s. (Courtesy of Ellenore Eddy Smith.)

Well-known horseman Noel Laing (at left) mingles with other hunters, including James Boyd (holding riding crop) at Southern Pines in the 1930s. The hunters are wearing the three different types of hats associated with fox hunting—the bowler, top hat, and hunting cap. (Courtesy of Ellenore Eddy Smith.)

A lone rider poses for Eddy along Broad Street, perhaps near the corner of New Hampshire Avenue in Southern Pines about 1920. (Courtesy of Ellenore Eddy Smith.)

For the majority of sportsmen who were unable to participate in the formal chasing of the fox, hunting for other wild game was a favorite pastime in the Sandhills during the early twentieth century. These bird dogs are pointing the way to quail or other prey for the hunter. (Courtesy of Gene Hamlin.)

Shown here is an early photograph of the Schemmler Building on Northeast Broad Street in Southern Pines in the 1910s. A German inventor named Schemmler erected the building in 1912. The Casino, as it was popularly called, contained a bowling alley and billiard tables. From 1921 until about 1950, Home Furnishing Company, a large furniture business, occupied the edifice. (Courtesy of First Savings Bank of Southern Pines.)

The small community of Lakeview lies in eastern Moore County on Crystal Lake. It was a popular recreational spot in the early twentieth century. Here a crowd is shown enjoying the view along the water's edge about 1920. (Courtesy of Gene Hamlin.)

Pictured in front of a grandstand in 1915 are members of the Pinebluff baseball team. The only piece of baseball equipment visible is a single bat, suggesting that the fielders may have played barehanded. (Courtesy of Willard E. Jones.)

These gentlemen enjoy a game of roque on a snow-covered court in Southern Pines. Roque, a more formalized version of croquet, is played with short-handled mallets. (Courtesy of Ellenore Eddy Smith.)

Shown above is a slightly elevated view of the tennis courts, with the municipal building of Southern Pines in the background. A few of the players stopped their game to pose for the camera. (Courtesy of Gene Hamlin.)

The clubhouse of the Southern Pines Country Club, completed in 1912, hosted many social activities outside the realm of golf. It had comfortable rooms for dining, meeting, and sitting. Here a crowd is shown relaxing on the porch about 1918. (Courtesy of Durwood Barbour.)

Five

Residences of the Natives

Landmarks (from left to right) visible in this 1910s real-photo postcard of McReynolds Street in Carthage are the Sinclair Brothers Building, a water tower, the Moore County Courthouse, and the grand home of Thomas Bethune Tyson II (1866–1924). The residence, completed in 1907, was a splendid example of the Colonial Revival style of architecture. (Courtesy of Willard E. Jones.)

C.C. Shaw (1781–1852), a farmer and turpentine dealer, built this house in the late 1830s on a large tract of land he purchased from John McNeill. The Moore County Historical Association purchased the Shaw House in 1946. The group restored the homestead and maintains it as a period museum at its original location at the corner of Morganton Road and Southwest Broad Street. Eddy photographed this scene before 1920. (Courtesy of Durwood Barbour.)

A Sandhills tourist mailed this postcard, made from an Eddy picture, of an unidentified African-American man posing at his cabin near Southern Pines, to Westfield, Massachusetts, on February 17, 1920. (Courtesy of Durwood Barbour.)

This ramshackled cabin just west of Southern Pines was the home of sharecropper "Uncle Ned" and his family. The shack was a favorite subject for Eddy postcards in the 1910s and 1920s. (Courtesy of Tony Parker.)

Ned's Family, near Southern Pines, N. C.

"Uncle Ned" and his family gather at the side of their shanty for this Eddy photograph, which appeared on a postcard before 1920. (Courtesy of Willard E. Jones.)

This magnificent mansion was the home of Henry Allison Page Sr. (1862–1935) in Aberdeen. Page was a son of Francis Allison Page and a brother of diplomat Walter Hines Page (1855–1918). Henry A. Page represented Moore County in the General Assembly and served as state food administrator during World War I. (Courtesy of Willard E. Jones.)

Here is an early photograph of the residence of Henry Allison Page Jr. (1887–1947) shortly after its construction in the early 1910s. Page was a prominent businessman and the president of the Cape Fear Railroad Company. Tragically, he drowned in a boating accident in Onslow County. The dwelling is still standing on Page's Hill in Aberdeen and is currently used as a bed-and-breakfast inn. (Courtesy of Willard E. Jones.)

James Boyd (d. 1910), a retired industrialist from Pennsylvania and grandfather of author James Boyd, built the original winter resort home called Weymouth (shown here in the 1910s) on his 2,500-acre estate in 1905. James and his brother, Jackson, later inherited the property, and in the early 1920s, architect Aymar Embury II redesigned and enlarged the home for James and his wife, Katherine Lamont Boyd (1896–1974). In 1979 the landmark was converted into the Weymouth Center for the Arts and Humanities. (Courtesy of Sarah M. Pope.)

Shown here is the entrance road and gatehouse of Weymouth at Southern Pines in the 1910s. James and Katherine Boyd resided in that structure while their redesigned mansion was being completed. While living in the gatehouse, James wrote and Katherine typed the manuscript for his first and most famous novel, *Drums*, which was published in 1925. (From the author's collection.)

An entire African-American farm family gathers by the road in front of its cabin near Southern Pines to pose for Eddy about 1920. At left a farmer walks behind a hand-held plow being pulled by an ox. In the distance boxcars are visible on the Seaboard Air Line Railroad. (Courtesy of Ellenore Eddy Smith.)

By the Sand Road, near Southern Pines, N. C.

Two African-American children tend to an iron pot in front of their family's cabin "by the sand road" in the vicinity of Southern Pines in 1914. To the right of the house is a small umbrella tree. (Courtesy of Durwood Barbour.)

A large tenant farm family stands next to its cabin alongside a census taker in 1920. The caption on the postcard reads, "No Sir! No Visitors here. Just the family home for Sunday Dinner." (Courtesy of Durwood Barbour.)

Eddy photographed this close-up portrait of an African-American family in Moore County near the entrance to their home about 1915. The grandparents standing on the far right of the picture postcard were probably former slaves. (Courtesy of Sarah M. Pope.)

Pictured here (c. 1928) is a distant view of "Blue Shutters," a Colonial Revival style house on Valley Road in eastern Southern Pines. Writer Hugh McNair Kahler built the dwelling as a simple shingle cottage in 1917, and a later owner enlarged the house. (Courtesy of Willard E. Jones.)

Arthur Ramsey of Washington, D.C., purchased the residence from Kahler in 1926 and modified it into its present elegant state. Perhaps Mr. and Mrs. Ramsey are the two people shown near the house in this close-up view. (Courtesy of Willard E. Jones.)

Six
Towns near the Resorts

Members of the fire department of Carthage conduct a demonstration during a drill near the Moore County Courthouse about 1915. The wooden interior of the courthouse was consumed by fire in 1889, but the brick walls survived and the structure was rebuilt the following year. (Courtesy of Willard E. Jones.)

Aberdeen was the first town in Moore County that Eddy encountered, arriving at the railroad station in the early morning hours of October 7, 1907. He returned to the municipality a few years later and took this photograph, which shows a portion of the depot (at left), the Aberdeen Hotel (right of center), the Aberdeen and Rockfish Railroad Depot (second from right), and the Bank of Aberdeen (far right). (Courtesy of Willard E. Jones.)

Pictured here is an early-1920s view of Aberdeen similar to the one shown above. The town was the leading railroad and industrial center in the county. By the time of this picture, automobiles had begun to replace horse-drawn conveyances. (From the author's collection.)

The buildings shown in this late-1910s photograph of Aberdeen are, left to right, the Aberdeen Hotel (1913), the Eva Page Building (1906), Aberdeen Hardware Company (1912), Page Trust Company (1914), the Aberdeen and Asheboro Railroad Office (1906), and Page Memorial Methodist Church (1913). (Courtesy of Ellenore Eddy Smith.)

Shown here is a c. 1910s postcard of historic Bethesda Presbyterian Church near Aberdeen. This structure was the third building of the congregation, which was established in 1788. Construction began in 1860 on the present-day church, and it was dedicated on May 10, 1862. The inscription on the message side of the postcard complimented Eddy: "It [the postcard] is just as I purchased it from Eddy's Studio in Southern Pines. He is supposed to carry the finest goods." (Courtesy of Willard E. Jones.)

Shown here is a postcard of the graded school at Aberdeen (c. 1920s). The brick building later served as Aberdeen High School, and subsequently the campus of the Aberdeen Middle School occupied the site. (Courtesy of Gene Hamlin.)

The fruit industry was an important part of the agricultural economy of Moore County in the early twentieth century. A local support group known as the Moore County Fruit Growers Association conducted its business in this building in Aberdeen. (Courtesy of Willard E. Jones.)

A large throng of people, some holding school banners, gathered near the courthouse square at Carthage on Friday, April 16, 1915, to participate in the Moore County schools commencement exercises. (Courtesy of Gene Hamlin.)

When E.C. Eddy first arrived in Pinehurst in 1907, photographic work was slow at Merrow's Studio, prompting Eddy to take his camera to Carthage. He stayed in a boarding home, because he probably could not afford to room at Tyson's Hotel (pictured here). Eddy earned $24 in four days. (Courtesy of Tony Parker.)

Court House.   Carthage, N. C.

The General Assembly incorporated the town of Carthage in 1796, and citizens constructed this substantial brick courthouse about 1840. Eddy photographed this view, looking up Monroe Street, about 1915. (Courtesy of Gene Hamlin.)

This postcard features a close-up view of the courthouse and the square about 1918. The county soon outgrew the building and replaced it in 1923. (Courtesy of Aubrey T. Haddock.)

The county erected this memorial after World War I at the old courthouse in honor of townsman James Rogers McConnell (1887–1917). He was a pilot with the Lafayette Escadrille and was shot down in aerial combat with German airplanes on March 19, 1917. (Courtesy of Gene Hamlin.)

Shown here is a ground-level view of the new three-story courthouse completed in 1923. The McConnell Memorial stands in front of the landmark, flanked by cannons and cannonballs. (From the author's collection.)

People enjoy some leisure time along the beach of Crystal Lake near the community of Lakeview in the 1920s. It was a favorite amusement spot in Moore County during warm weather in the early part of the century. (Courtesy of Gene Hamlin.)

Crystal Spring was located on the property of Piney Woods Inn in Southern Pines. Eddy reproduced the springhouse on a postcard in the mid-1910s. The spring provided therapeutic water for visitors to the hotel. (Courtesy of Aubrey T. Haddock.)

Seven

Wagons, Oxcarts, Carriages, and the *Buzz Buzzard*

On January 12, 1914, Eddy made this photograph of Will McNulty and his donkey "Joe" in front of the Southern Pines Hotel. The pair was traveling from Syracuse, New York, to Jacksonville, Florida. The banner held by McNulty indicated that the duo hoped to appear in 1915 at the Panama Pacific International Exposition (world's fair), to be held in San Francisco, California. (Courtesy of Sarah M. Pope.)

Inhabitants of Southern Pines celebrated Schooner Day as an annual event for many years. Participants rode in a parade of wagons through the town. (Courtesy of Sarah M. Pope.)

These farmers have arrived by wagon at Southern Pines with produce and farm products to barter and sell at the local market. Eddy observed that many of the natives were still riding into town in schooner wagons and oxcarts before 1920. (Courtesy of Sarah M. Pope.)

A team of yoked oxen pulls a loaded farm wagon along a dirt road "on the way to market" near Southern Pines about 1915. (Courtesy of Durwood Barbour.)

Two African-American boys pause for Eddy's camera in route to the market in Southern Pines. Livestock served as their means of transportation. (Courtesy of Sarah M. Pope.)

A pair of mules harnessed to a schooner wagon awaits the return trip to the farm. One of the animals, identified as "Tired Tim," takes full advantage of the rest on Broad Street in Southern Pines about 1915. (From the author's collection.)

These natives have hitched a farm animal to their crude cart to transport them near Southern Pines in the 1910s. Hay is a substitute fuel for gasoline, as the caption jokes, "hay burner—three miles to the gallon." (Courtesy of Gene Hamlin.)

Eddy photographed this African-American man at the reins of his primitive bull-driven cart near Southern Pines in the 1910s. The wheels of the vehicle are caked with mud. (Courtesy of Durwood Barbour.)

Four local children strike a fetching pose atop this farm animal near Pinehurst in the 1910s. An older girl peers out at the camera from an opening in a log building. The postcard is captioned "on the way to town." (Courtesy of Sarah M. Pope.)

A distinguished old couple rides in a bull-drawn carriage at Southern Pines between 1915 and 1920. The gentleman holds a whip in his hand, and the woman wears a small bouquet of flowers. (Courtesy of Durwood Barbour.)

Eddy focuses on a Red Cross truck moving north along Broad Street in an Armistice Day parade in Southern Pines about 1921. The man standing in the back of the vehicle is Dr. James S. Milliken. (Courtesy of First Savings Bank of Southern Pines.)

In 1910 Eddy photographed his daughter Doris, and his wife, Alice, in a buggy on its way from Pinehurst to Southern Pines. The vehicle is crossing a small wooden bridge in the vicinity of Pinehurst. Eddy described the roads outside the village as sand trails. (Courtesy of Ellenore Eddy Smith.)

A flatbed truck of a motor company operated by Henry A. Page Jr. of Aberdeen is parked near the Princess Theater in Southern Pines about 1920. Page was one of the most prominent businessmen in the county after World War I. (Courtesy of Ellenore Eddy Smith.)

Shown here is an aircraft of the Colonial Aerial Transportation Company in 1920. Eddy boarded the plane and took aerial views of Southern Pines. (Courtesy of Ellenore Eddy Smith.)

Pictured above is another view of the biplane in which Eddy flew to make bird's-eye views of his town in 1920. An unidentified man observes the takeoff. (Courtesy of Ellenore Eddy Smith.)

An unidentified photographer took this image of Eddy getting assistance with his headgear just prior to his aerial assignment in 1920. Eddy needed fresh air after the flight because the fumes from the airplane almost made him sick. (Courtesy of Ellenore Eddy Smith.)

A crowd of onlookers stares intently at a large biplane on the ground at Pinehurst in the early 1910s. The man on the right appears to be taking a photograph of the airplane. (Courtesy of Ellenore Eddy Smith.)

Automobiles are parked along the rail during a trotting race at the Pinehurst track in the late 1910s. When Eddy first arrived at Pinehurst in 1908, Leonard Tufts owned the only car in the village. (Courtesy of Ellenore Eddy Smith.)

Just prior to his retirement, Eddy made this photograph of the Moore County Chapter of the American Red Cross car in the early 1940s. Two of the women standing beside the automobile are society members Audrey Kennedy and Barbara Bellamy. (Courtesy of First Savings Bank of Southern Pines.)

Eight
Agriculture

The production of cotton was historically more important in the states of the Deep South than in North Carolina. However, farmers raised cotton in many eastern counties of the state, including Moore County, in the early twentieth century. Cotton fields made popular landscapes for photographers such as Eddy, who hailed from the North. (Courtesy of Willard E. Jones.)

Eddy published this charming postcard of African-American children in a cotton field near Southern Pines in 1914. Cotton was one of several major crops grown in Moore County at that time. (Courtesy of Willard E. Jones.)

In the following three photographs made into postcards, the same three children acted as models in a cotton patch for Eddy in 1914. Here the young people are seated in front of a pile of cotton. (Courtesy of Sarah M. Pope.)

In this sprightly photograph titled "Sunny South," Eddy placed the smiling children behind a mound of cotton balls. (Courtesy of Gene Hamlin.)

Finally, the photographer persuaded the children to recline on a mound of cotton to produce this restful, but uncommon scene in a cotton field. (Courtesy of Gene Hamlin.)

Ellenore Eddy Smith notes that this 1914 photograph of a cotton field near a tenant farmhouse at Southern Pines was one of her father's favorite views. (Courtesy of Sarah M. Pope.)

These laborers picking cotton in a large field near Southern Pines demonstrate the back-breaking work associated with the crop. (Courtesy of Sarah M. Pope.)

This crude bull-powered conveyance transports a farmer along a dirt road near a thatched-roof outbuilding outside of Southern Pines. (Courtesy of Ellenore Eddy Smith.)

With the aid of an ox, a local farmer plows a field near his home in the 1910s. This Kodak photograph may have been intended for one of Eddy's picture postcards. He produced photographs of interesting subjects that he believed tourists would like to mail back home. (Courtesy of Ellenore Eddy Smith.)

Eddy placed this elevated view of a dewberry field near Southern Pines on a postcard prior to World War I. The message on the reverse side of the card was dated March 29, 1916. (Courtesy of B.T. Fowler.)

African-American dewberry pickers pose in a large field in Moore County. The fruit was an important crop during the first quarter of the twentieth century and was abundantly grown in the eastern portions of the county near Cameron. (Courtesy of Sarah M. Pope.)

A dirt road intersects a peach orchard in bloom near Southern Pines about 1920. Peaches were a significant part of the agricultural economy of the Sandhills at that time. (Courtesy of Gene Hamlin.)

These three workers are picking peaches in an orchard near Southern Pines before 1915. Cold weather and disease often limited the peach harvest. (Courtesy of Durwood Barbour.)

One of the important early industries of the county was the distillation of resin from longleaf pines into turpentine. Enterprising farmers illegally used a similar process to make moonshine whiskey. Here a man stokes the fire of a still near Southern Pines. (Courtesy of Gene Hamlin.)

This landmark, photographed by Eddy in the 1930s, is McKenzie's Mill near Pinehurst. By the time of this visit, the old gristmill was in dire need of restoration. The structure is no longer standing. (Courtesy of First Savings Bank of Southern Pines.)

Nine

Famous and Anonymous Faces

The E.L. Merrow Studio of Pinehurst published this postcard of a large crowd assembled at the gun club at Pinehurst (probably in January 1909) to watch famous sharpshooter Annie Oakley (1860–1926) perform a shooting exhibition. (Courtesy of Durwood Barbour.)

Annie Oakley and her husband, Frank Butler, visited Pinehurst on several occasions between 1909 and 1923. Several men are assisting Oakley in a fancy-shooting demonstration before an attentive audience at the gun club. Her grand finale was breaking four clay balls tossed in the air at the same time by her husband. (Courtesy of Tufts Archives, Pinehurst.)

A group of spectators views a shooting match at the gun club at Pinehurst about 1910. In the back row, to the right of the man who is standing, are Doris and Alice Eddy. At least two members of the audience are holding Kodak cameras. The man holding the camera in the front row may be E.L. Merrow. (Courtesy of Ellenore Eddy Smith.)

Lincoln Beachey, early exhibition pilot, brought his Curtiss biplane to Pinehurst in March 1911. Here, onlookers line both sides of the runway near the aviation tent in anticipation of the first airplane flight in Moore County. (Courtesy of Tufts Archives, Pinehurst.)

Beachey sits at the controls of his Curtiss "pusher" in a field at Pinehurst in March 1911. Beachey assembled the airplane from a combination of bamboo, wooden struts, and wire. (Courtesy of Tufts Archives, Pinehurst.)

Strapped in a seat to the right of Beachey is amateur golf champion Charles "Chick" Evans Jr. (1890–1979). After Evans defeated Walter J. Travis (1862–1927) in the North and South Amateur Tournament in 1911, Beachey offered to take him for a flight. Evans admitted to being nervous before the ascent but while in the air "felt as safe as if sitting upon a sheltered balcony." (Courtesy of Ellenore Eddy Smith.)

Pictured here with Beachey is Commander S. Saito of the Royal Japanese Navy. The unidentified man at right is about to start the airplane's motor by spinning the propeller by hand. The foreign passenger enjoyed two flights in Beachey's *Buzz Buzzard* in early April 1911. Saito was excited about the aircraft and realized its potential for use by the Japanese military. (Courtesy of Tufts Archives, Pinehurst.)

Com. S Saito, Jap. Navy   At Pinehurst N.C.

While visiting Pinehurst in the spring of 1911, Saito was one of the few lucky individuals to fly with Beachey. Here a band of dignitaries poses with the airplane before the flight. (Courtesy of Ellenore Eddy Smith.)

Commander Saito exhibits a wide grin in reaction to the start of the motor and movement of the airplane just prior to takeoff. (Courtesy of Ellenore Eddy Smith.)

The purposes of Beachey's visit to Pinehurst were to give flying lessons as well as to conduct exhibition flights. On March 21, Miss E. Marie Sinclair, a sportswoman from New York, received a ride in Beachey's aircraft. (Courtesy of Tufts Archives, Pinehurst.)

Shown here is a close-up view of a confident Miss Sinclair seated beside Beachey. The daring female athlete was treated to a long and high flight. Sinclair was the only woman, other than Beachey's wife, to fly during the pilot's appearance at Pinehurst. (Courtesy of Ellenore Eddy Smith.)

These patriotically decorated floats were on display in the parade of the Firemen's Carnival in Southern Pines in March 1915. The horse-drawn vehicle represented the Southern Pines Gun Club. (Courtesy of Gene Hamlin.)

These Boy Scouts are lining up to march in the parade of the Firemen's Carnival in March 1915 in Southern Pines. The information on the message side of the postcard reveals that the scouts had recently purchased new uniforms with money earned from a play. The fifth boy from the left is John Ruggles. (Courtesy of Gene Hamlin.)

A large assemblage of former slaveholders and their descendants from Moore County gathers in a public park in Southern Pines in the mid-1930s for the annual commemoration known as Old Slave Day. The town inaugurated the event in April 1934. (Courtesy of Ellenore Eddy Smith.)

This unidentified former slave is pictured here with her ox-drawn cart at an Old Slave Day event at Southern Pines in the 1930s. She proudly stands before the camera, smoking a pipe and wearing her name tag. The Park View Hotel (formerly the Juneau) is visible in the background. (Courtesy of Ellenore Eddy Smith.)

These two elderly gentlemen who appeared at Old Slave Day are the Reverend Thomas B. McCain (1853–1939) and possibly Demus Taylor. McCain (on the left) was a retired minister of the African Methodist Episcopal Church and a leading figure in Southern Pines. Taylor was said to be more than 100 years old and was a well-known turpentine worker in Moore County. (Courtesy of Ellenore Eddy Smith.)

About 50 former slaves and their descendants pose for Eddy at the park in Southern Pines in the mid-1930s. These elderly citizens assembled annually in April to feast on a lunch prepared by the town, sing spirituals, listen to an old-fashioned sermon, and reminisce about the old days.

Southern Pines was the only town in the state to pay tribute to former slaves. (Courtesy of Ellenore Eddy Smith.)

Among Eddy's numerous golf-related photographs is this portrait of Charles "Chick" Evans Jr. in 1911. At that time Evans was a rising star in the realm of amateur golf. He won the United States Open and United States Amateur championships in 1916 and was a member of the Walker Cup Team three times during the 1920s. Evans competed in the United States Amateur Championship 50 times and is a member of the Golf Hall of Fame. (Courtesy of Tufts Archives, Pinehurst.)

Australian-born Walter J. Travis was the first prominent golfer to develop his game in the United States. Shown here with his trademark cigar, Travis tees off during a tournament at Pinehurst. The date is likely 1910, one of the years that he won the North and South Amateur Tournament. (Courtesy of Ellenore Eddy Smith.)

Surly Walter J. Travis smiles at fellow competitor Paul M. Hunter of Midlothian, Illinois, after defeating him in the seventh annual Holiday Week Golf Tournament at Pinehurst in December 1910. Hunter lost the match by missing a short putt on the 17th hole. (Courtesy of Tufts Archives, Pinehurst.)

This photogenic little fellow, dressed in a sailor suit, serves as a willing model for Eddy in this striking portrait. (Courtesy of Ellenore Eddy Smith.)

Eddy photographed this distinguished-looking African-American woman at his studio in Southern Pines about 1920. The Southern Pines *Pilot* ran the photograph in a recent edition in hopes of determining the identity of the woman. (Courtesy of Ellenore Eddy Smith.)

Colonel E.S. Knight and his trained
eagle strike a profile pose for Eddy at
Southern Pines in the 1930s. The bird
is perched on the trainer's arm, and
Knight is seated on the eagle's wooden
cage. Knight was affiliated with the
Chautauqua program that visited the
local Congregational church. (Courtesy
of Ellenore Eddy Smith.)

Gutzon Borglum (1867–1941), the renowned
sculptor and painter, paid an occasional visit
to the Sandhills region. Eddy took this
portrait of him in the 1920s. (Courtesy of
Ellenore Eddy Smith.)

This distinguished group of men posed for Eddy in the 1920s. Left to right are Gutzon Borglum, ? Fuller, ? Fuller (father of the former), and an unidentified associate of the elder Fuller. Two of Borglum's major works are the Mount Rushmore Memorial and the Confederate Memorial on Stone Mountain. (Courtesy of Ellenore Eddy Smith.)

During several fall seasons, Eddy undertook an assignment to photograph noted Pinehurst golf course designer Donald J. Ross playing on one of his layouts. Here, Ross attempts a chip shot over water to a slightly elevated green.

Here, Ross assumes his putting stance on one of the sand greens. The photographs were used in a calendar produced by Pinehurst and, according to Eddy, required that he achieve perfect detail in the entire picture. (Courtesy of Tufts Archives, Pinehurst.)

This "gentleman rider of experience" is talented novelist James Boyd. Here he is dressed as master of the foxhounds, with brass-buttoned coat, black hunting cap, horn to signal the hounds, riding crop, and white gloves. This Eddy photograph was taken from a painting of Boyd. (Courtesy of First Savings Bank of Southern Pines.)

This postcard shows James Boyd (left) and Jackson H. Boyd, joint masters of the Moore County Hounds, beginning a hunt west of the kennels at Weymouth in the 1930s. (Courtesy of Bob W. Brendle.)

This handsome creature is a local hunting dog photographed by Eddy in a pointing position. (Courtesy of Ellenore Eddy Smith.)

Index

This Eddy vertical-format postcard depicts a sand road cut through the pine forest near Southern Pines. (Courtesy of B.T. Fowler.)

Near Southern Pines, N. C.

When The Dogwood Blooms The Longleaf Pi
So. Pines N
© 1914 By E.C. Eddy

Eddy published this artistic view of dogwood blossoms entangled with a pine tree in the spring of 1914. (Courtesy of Durwood Barbour.)

This large umbrella tree grows in close proximity to a home in Southern Pines in the 1910s. (Courtesy of Durwood Barbour.)

Eddy reproduced this close-up image of a longleaf pine branch on a postcard in the 1930s. (Courtesy of Gene Hamlin.)